CONTENTS

Words in the glossary are in **bold** the first time they appear in the text.

SCHOOLCHILDREN

World War Two began when Nazi Germany invaded Poland on 1 September 1939. This led to Britain and France declaring war against Germany on 3 September. The war caused a lot of change and upset for schools.

Schoolchildren at that time had a very different life from children at schools today. Pupils sat at wooden desks with lift-up lids and ink-wells to dip their pens into. Classrooms did not have central heating. **Coke** stoves heated the classrooms in the winter, but they were still very cold.

Silence in class! 1939
Children queue up to have their maths work marked by the teacher.

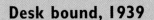

Desk bound, 1939
Pupils sit at their wooden desks in an art lesson. The windows in this classroom were so high up that children could see only the sky out of them.

GAS ATTACK?

When the war began, people were afraid that Germany would drop poison gas bombs on Britain. The government gave out 38 million gas masks, and everyone had to carry their gas mask at all times.

Children had to take their gas mask to school every day. They practised putting them on in class. The gas masks were made of rubber and smelt funny. In fact, the Germans never used gas bombs and people gave up carrying gas masks.

It's a gas, 1941
A teacher shows her class how to put on a gas mask.
'We all had black ones except my little sister. She had a red one with a red nose on it that flapped up and down.' (Jean Carberry)

Gas practice, 1941
A crowd of schoolchildren practise what to do should a poison gas bomb be dropped.

I REMEMBER ....
'The school windows had sticky tape criss-crossed over them to stop the glass from shattering everywhere if a bomb dropped nearby.'
.... (Joyce, Biggleswade)

EVACUATION

Large towns and cities were heavily bombed in the war. The government evacuated millions of children from the cities to safer parts of the country.

Whole schools were evacuated, including the teachers. Sometimes it was difficult to find somewhere to set up the school again. Often the evacuated school had to share a building with the school in the safer area. The two schools took turns to use the classrooms – one had lessons in the morning, the other in the afternoon.

Leaving the city, 1939
Evacuees queue to board trains. Thousands of children left London for safer areas of the country.

Meeting Auntie, 1939
Evacuees meet their **foster mother** for the first time. Anyone with a spare bedroom was expected to look after an evacuee. Going to live with strangers was frightening for many children.

School at the palace, 1939
A group of evacuees hard at work. Their school moved into the Bishop of Chichester's palace in West Sussex during the war.

LEARNING FROM LIFE

Children learned a lot from evacuation. People from cities met people from the countryside, and they learned about each other.

In some schools, teachers mixed the evacuees and the local children together. Many city children had never been to the country before and some did not know where milk came from. Teachers took their evacuees on nature walks. When one child saw cows for the first time he said, 'Miss, whatever are those? Horses with handlebars?'

London songs, 1941
Four evacuees from east London teach their new classmates a song. Some classes became very full when schools joined together.

A class cut, 1939
A teacher gives her pupil a haircut! Teachers had to do more than just teach the evacuees who were living away from home.

Evacuee excursion, 1940
A teacher takes some evacuees for a walk. Teachers tried to find things for pupils to do after school, to stop them from getting into mischief in their foster homes.

THE BLITZ

From September 1940 to May 1941 there were air raids on Britain every night. German aircraft flew over London and other cities and dropped bombs. This was called the Blitz.

Schools had to have **air-raid shelters** in case there was an **air raid** during schooltime. Children spent many miserable hours in cold, damp air-raid shelters singing and chanting their times tables. Some had to run to their air-raid shelters so often the teachers counted it as exercise and did not bother much with PE lessons.

Back to school, 1940
Children leave their concrete air-raid shelters after a practice alarm. About one school in every five in London was damaged by bombing.

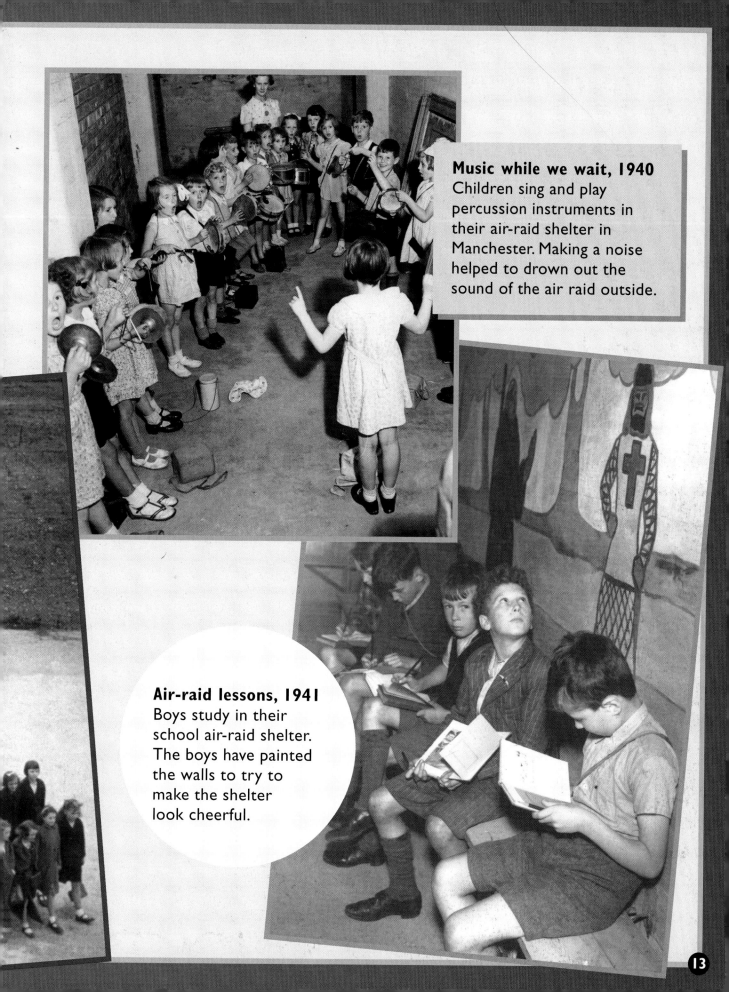

Music while we wait, 1940
Children sing and play percussion instruments in their air-raid shelter in Manchester. Making a noise helped to drown out the sound of the air raid outside.

Air-raid lessons, 1941
Boys study in their school air-raid shelter. The boys have painted the walls to try to make the shelter look cheerful.

CITY SCHOOLS

Many evacuees were so unhappy that they went home. But back home in the cities, there wasn't always a school for them to attend.

A lot of school buildings were taken over by **air-raid wardens**, or used as **rest centres** for people whose homes had been bombed. Groups of children were taught at home by teachers who visited them for a couple of hours a day, and left them with homework.

Pump attendant, 1939
A young evacuee living at a garage helps to fill a car with petrol. Some children, who had no school to go to, took on a job.

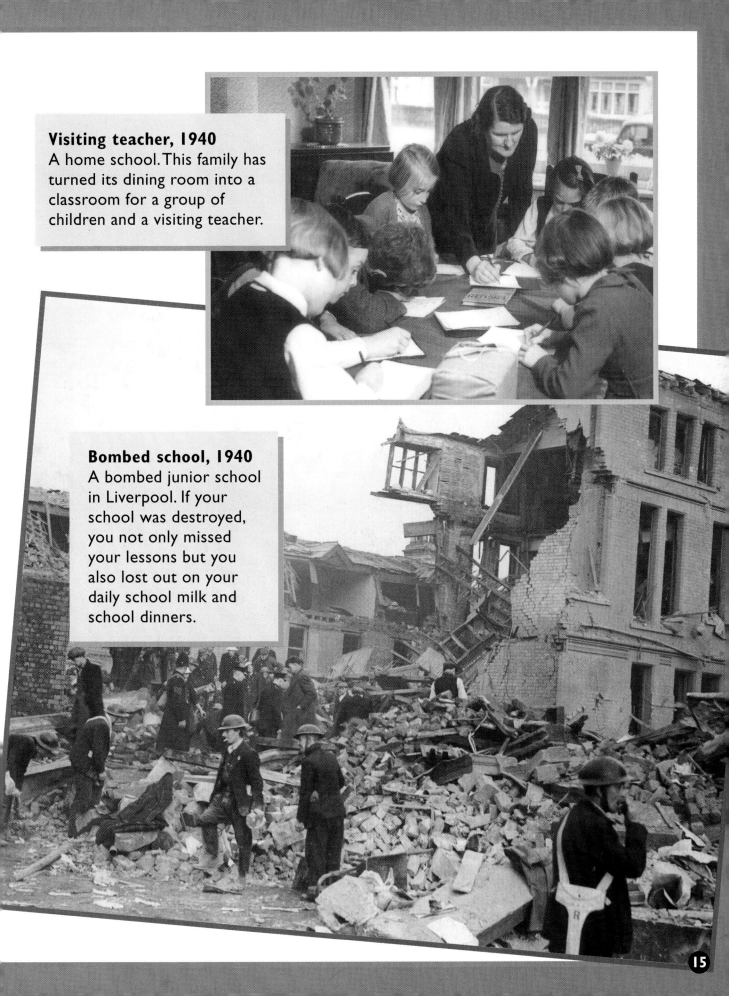

Visiting teacher, 1940
A home school. This family has turned its dining room into a classroom for a group of children and a visiting teacher.

Bombed school, 1940
A bombed junior school in Liverpool. If your school was destroyed, you not only missed your lessons but you also lost out on your daily school milk and school dinners.

MISSED LESSONS

Teachers did their best to keep schools open, but all over the country children missed a lot of lessons for many different reasons.

Children had to go to air-raid shelters at night during the Blitz. Sometimes they were so tired at school the next day that they were allowed to put their heads down on their desks for a sleep. Some children did not go to school because they had to stay at home to look after younger brothers or sisters. Others stayed at home because their school had been hit by a bomb, or because their teacher had left and joined the army.

Bomb-site, 1945
Young children play in the ruins of a bombed-out house instead of going to school. A lot of children collected the **fins of incendiaries** as trophies. Sometimes they accidentally picked up **unexploded bombs**.

Blitz swing, 1943
Children play on a **bombsite**.
When schools were closed,
many children ran wild on
bomb-sites, which were
dangerous places to play.

I REMEMBER ·······················
'The nightly raids meant that even though we had
beds in the shelter we didn't get much sleep.'
······································· (Boy, London)

SCHOOL FOOD

School milk and school dinners helped to keep Britain's children healthy during the war years. At break-time every morning, children were given a third of a pint of milk to drink.

Not many schools provided hot dinners when the war started. Most children went home for lunch. The government wanted more schools to give hot dinners and, by the end of the war, a third of all schoolchildren ate school dinners. Most schools grew their own vegetables, and cooked them for lunch.

School milk, 1940
Primary school girls drink their daily bottle of milk. School milk was free for the poorest children.

School dinner, 1941
Children line up for their school dinner. Poor children got their dinners free. This was the best meal of the day for many children.

I REMEMBER ....
'When the school milk was delivered in the morning it was put next to the coke stove so that it was warm at break-time. How yellow the cream was!'
.... (Sheila, aged 5)

CHANGING LESSONS

**The dreadful bombing of the Blitz stopped in 1941.
Schools settled down again but school timetables changed.**

Lessons now included things like growing vegetables, how to mend clothes and pig-keeping. These were important activities during the war. Schools could not always provide much sport. For PE, pupils often just stood in lines in the playground and did a few exercises. Clothes **rationing** meant that children did not usually have a change of clothes or shoes for PE.

Darning socks, 1940
Boys learn how to **darn** socks. Clothes were rationed, so you had to mend your clothes if they got a hole in them.

Dig for Victory, 1939
Children work in the school garden. Inside, other children work hard in the classroom.

I REMEMBER ••••••••••••••••••••••••••••••••••••••
'We had swimming lessons in an outdoor pool near the school. I remember the air-raid siren once sounded when we were actually in the water. There was a mad dash for the air-raid shelters. We were all dripping wet and got very cold before the all-clear sounded.'

(Jenny, Lewes)

UNIFORMS

**Most primary schools did not have a uniform.
Boys wore shorts and long socks all the year round,
and girls wore skirts.**

Older children usually did wear a uniform, even though it was
difficult to buy a school uniform because of clothes rationing.
Everyone had a clothes ration book with **coupons** in it. To
buy a dress or coat you needed 25 coupons, 18 coupons for
shirts and jumpers, and 20 coupons for shoes.

Jumping the waves, 1939
Schoolgirl evacuees enjoy a
paddle in the sea, wearing
their school uniform.

Taking the register, 1939
While the teacher is away, two older girls take the register for a class of infants. One little girl is wearing her Brownie uniform – maybe she had no other clothes to wear that day?

I REMEMBER..............
'Once rationing began, our school didn't worry about whether or not we were wearing our uniform.'
.... (Roy, Brighton)

PLAYTIME

Children played traditional games in the playground, such as singing, skipping and ball games. Marbles, hopscotch and 'cowboys and Indians' were always popular, too.

They played different games at different times of the year – conkers in the autumn, **whip and top** in the winter, handstands and cartwheels in the summer. Children brought long skipping ropes to school. Two of them turned the rope while their friends ran in and jumped over it, and everyone chanted rhymes.

Playground skip, 1944
Skipping in the playground. It took skill for a group of six girls to skip together like this.

Easter marbles, 1941
Boys use Easter eggs for their game of marbles.

Conkers galore, 1942
Schoolboys with their conker collection. They collected the conkers to play with and for farmers, who used conkers to feed their cows.

HARVEST-TIME

Many men had gone away to war, so women and children had to help out on farms. At harvest-time, thousands of schoolchildren had a change from lessons and went to help farmers with the harvest.

Children were taken on a lorry to the farm and usually spent the day collecting potatoes or picking fruit. It was hard work, but great fun. Some children stayed on farm harvest camps, having a working holiday. Children over 12 years old who lived on farms were allowed to have time off school to help during the harvest.

Gardeners' march, 1939
Gardening and farm work were normal parts of school life for many children.

Potato pickers, 1943
Evacuated schoolgirls collect potatoes. Most children thought that going to a farm instead of going to school was a great treat.

I REMEMBER ....

'Schooldays were awful, but I could escape by volunteering for potato-picking. I'd turn up for school in old ragged clothes, get my name ticked off, and then grab the back seat of the coach...The tractor dug the spuds up, and we filled the sacks.'

.... (Boy, Coventry)

WAR ENDS

The war in Europe ended in 1945. Teachers who had joined the armed forces came home and went back to their classrooms. Damaged schools were rebuilt.

The war had made the government realise how poor some people were. Evacuation had shown the big differences between people who lived in the city and people who lived in the country. The government wanted to make things fairer, and to make schools better for all children.

Back from war, 1945
Boys at a **secondary school** learn geography. After the war, the age when children could leave school was raised from 14 to 15 years old.

Room for improvement, 1948
Schoolboys do PE in the spacious hall of a new secondary school. After the war, lots of new schools with modern equipment were built.

I REMEMBER ....
'Even after the war ended some things were still not in the shops. We played rounders and tennis at school, but it was hard to find a tennis racquet to buy.'
.... (Madge, aged 12)

GLOSSARY

Air raid a sudden attack from the air, such as the nightly attacks on Britain by German planes during the Blitz (1940-41)

Air-raid shelters safe places for people to go during an air raid

Air-raid wardens people given the job of helping everyone in their street or area during an air raid. They could give first-aid to the injured.

Armed forces the forces to protect a country: its army, air force and navy

Blitz the heavy bombing of Britain's towns, factories and railways by German planes in the early war years

Bomb-site the ruins of a building or place where a bomb has dropped

Coke a fuel like coal

Coupon a piece of paper which can be exchanged in a shop for things you want to buy

Darn mend holes in clothes

Evacuee People sent away for safety. Children and mothers with babies that lived in the most dangerous areas were sent to live somewhere safer.

Fins of incendiaries the steel fins of an incendiary bomb (fire bomb) that were left after the bomb had burned away.

Foster mother a woman who looked after evacuated children. Foster mothers were often called 'Auntie' by evacuees.

Gas mask a mask that allows you to breathe without being poisoned if there is poison gas in the air

Rationing allowing an equal share to everyone. Things that were in short supply, like food, clothing and petrol, were all rationed.

Rest centres places for people to go to when their homes had been destroyed by bombs. They gave basic food and shelter.

Secondary schools schools for children who were over 11 years old

Traditional describes something that is handed down from one generation to another, such as songs, games and customs

Unexploded bomb a bomb that fails to blow up (explode) when it lands, but might still blow up if it is moved

Whip and top a game with a spinning top that children set spinning by using a stick with a heavy cord tied to it. They tried to keep the top spinning by whipping it.

FURTHER INFORMATION

Books

Butterfield, Moira, *Going to War in World War Two* (Franklin Watts, 2001)

Cooper, Alison, *Rationing* (Hodder Wayland, 2003)

Deary, Terry, *Horrible History, The Woeful Second World War* (Hippo, 1999)

Hamley, Dennis, *The Second World War* (Franklin Watts, 2004)

Masters, Anthony, *World War II Stories* (Franklin Watts, 2004)

Parsons, Martin, *Britain at War: Rationing* (Wayland, 1999)

Reynoldson, Fiona, *The Past in Pictures: The Home Front* (Wayland, 1999)

Reynoldson, Fiona, *What Families Were Like: The Second World War* (Hodder Wayland, 2002)

Websites

The Home Front section of the Spartacus Second World War Encyclopedia: http://www.spartacus.schoolnet.co.uk/2WWhome.htm

Fun interactive BBC site, in which you can pretend to go shopping in wartime Britain, read letters from evacuees and hear the sound of an air-raid warning: http://www.bbc.co.uk/history/ww2children//index.shtml

Home Sweet Home Front site containing useful information, and interesting photos and posters on various key topics: rationing, Dig for Victory, land girls, evacuees, squander: http://www.homesweethomefront.co.uk/templates/hshf_frameset_tem.htm

The Second World War Experience Centre site, with descriptions of aspects of life on the home front, and memories from those who experienced it: http://www.war-experience.org/history/keyaspects/home-british/

Wartime Memories Project. An interactive site containing questions to and answers from people who lived through World War Two: http://www.wartimememories.co.uk/questions.html

Note to parents and teachers

Every effort has been made by the Publishers to ensure that these websites are suitable for children; that they are of the highest educational value, and that they contain no inappropriate or offensive material. However, because of the nature of the Internet, it is impossible to guarantee that the contents of these sites will not be altered. We strongly advise that Internet access is supervised by a responsible adult.

INDEX

Thanks to the following for permission to quote from their sources: (p. 5) the Wartime Memories Project; (p. 6) *No Time To Wave Goodbye* by Ben Wicks, Bloomsbury Publishing Ltd.; (pp. 17, 27) *Children of the Blitz* by Robert Westall, Macmillan Children's Books, London, UK.